Anatomy of a New York Debut Recital

a Chronicle

by Carol Montparker

Preface

When this Chronicle was being recorded eight years ago, it was entirely for my own comfort and catharsis, with no thought at all of "sharing" it; but I casually showed it to a friend who, in turn, gave it to the publisher of a music magazine.* I was flabbergasted when he asked me if he could print it. Not only was the journal incomplete, (the recital had not yet taken place), but I had to consider seriously whether I was willing to publicly bare my innermost thoughts and feelings.

The decision being made, neither the publisher not I could possibly have anticipated the rush of response from hundreds of readers. "Closet pianists" came out and presented debuts writing letters of thanks for the "heartening and refreshing knowledge that they were not alone" with their doubts and fears; music teachers wrote that they were making it "must" reading for serious students; athletes and other performers wrote of parallel emotions; and some quite distinguished and renowned pianists wrote, reconfirming that at all levels of success, the same emotional and aesthetic sensations are encountered.

Copies of the original publication have long since run out, and requests for reprints up till the present have encouraged us to think that by simply being open and honest something of value might have emerged.

C.M.

* * *

(Some portions herein have never been printed before.)
First published in The Piano Quarterly, Summer 1976

Introduction

A story of my several months' preparation for a New York "debut" recital would be impossible without references to those who were most closely involved with me at the time.

My husband, a musician himself, was a relentlessly severe yet honest critic, who lived with a good case of overexposure to the program and its built-in tensions, yet managed to support and encourage me through this "project."

My son Dennis and daughter Kim, gifted and serious cellist and flutist respectively, and educated listeners, shared all the excitement of the event with me. An occasional "That sounded great, Mom!" in the middle of a dreary practice session was more meaningful to me than a hundred *N.Y. Times* reviews.

To my wonderful teacher and friend, Josef Fidelman, I owe a huge debt of gratitude. He has taught me to approach the music in his scholarly and meticulous fashion, has been a fount of insights into the essential elements of Music and Piano-playing, and his own superb playing and recordings have been a great source of inspiration. Along with all of this, his loyal, loving and supporting nature has never ceased to encourage me when my spirits flagged.

To the late Leopold ("Lully") Mittman, my former teacher and close friend for over twenty years, a beautiful pianist and painter, I will be ever grateful for filling my most impressionable formative years with rich artistic visions and awakening my soul to so many of the creative wonders of the world.

Thanks to my parents, who were astute enough to recognize my musical needs at the earliest stages and provide me with the finest education though it wasn't always easy. My mother was my first teacher, and my father is, hands down, my most constant and tireless audience.

This would also be the time to thank my beautiful friends for their belief in me, their cheering words and actions, and keen perceptions from which I must draw. They know who they are.

A CHRONICLE

Carol Montparker

What finally made me take the plunge? Conversations with and support from loving friends? A slow ripening and awareness of inevitable pianistic currents? Am I a "late bloomer" for whom the time was just ripe; or did my other submerged self step momentarily outside of the conscious me and dial the phone to make the final commitment: rent the hall, engage the manager, sign my next few months away to a monastic existence which I don't even know if I can sustain. . . . ?

Probably all of the above. But here I am, alternately euphoric and hyper-stimulated by the exciting prospects ahead, and victim of deathly nervous tensions while wheeling the cart in the super-market. The only safe place for me now is at the piano, and maybe I have been running away from it too long.

Tiny worrisome details. Is one who has children in school capable of guiltlessly taking the phone off the hook for four hours a day so the practicing rolls smoothly undisturbed? Or, will the guilt itself be an impediment to a pure practice session? Will I, at this late stage, be able to develop sounder, more conservative practice habits, and not "give a performance" each time I sit down? Would Yoga and transcendental meditation help me to relax and facilitate concentration? How will I determine what the final program will be? Isn't it true that I should play only that which I would perform with love, without considering trends, gimmicks, or critics' tastes? How do I divorce myself from the preoccupation with critiques? What should the encores be? Will I *need* encores?

May I dare to consider my readings as valid as established recordings of great artists even if mine are quite different? Does one stay away from interpreting the "giant" (Beethoven) because critics have implied that he is to be touched by the so-called great only? How can I manage to keep confidence I only feel with the keyboard under my fingers, wherever I go?

How can I muster up that certain sensual feeling in the fingertips — which is the only way to project a deep delicious tone — any time of the day, on any piano, at will?

How will I draw and learn to savor the essence and nuances of a strange piano and give a successful program on an instrument on which one scant hour is all that is granted beforehand — not even enough time to play everything through once?

Will a crossword puzzle backstage, in the little sterile chamber which echoes one's heartbeats, be enough to harness my nerves?

Will friends understand my new preoccupation, sudden unavailability and impatience with interruptions? Will they wait for me until February? Will February be the end? Do I want it to be a beginning? What am I trying to prove? To whom?

Millions of details and questions keep cropping up, the analyses of which would only forestall the practice itself. The answers will come in the months ahead, and between the keyboard and the pen, perhaps I will keep a cool enough head to survive the experience with all sorts of new perceptions and insights as well as a measure of fulfillment.

* * *

Two more days left before school opens: my psychological starting line for digging in, and two days left of the vacation I bestowed upon myself, for indulgence and all frivolous excuses for not practicing. And then how to begin?

Is there anyone I haven't telephoned with my momentous piece of news? There's no backing out now. I'm in a new ballpark, and how I got there is no longer the issue.

* * *

It's down to Basics and the paring off of all non-essential time-devourers like birdwatching, sun-worshipping, garage sales, flea markets, needlework, rap sessions, and even the beloved water-colors.

As though the script were written for this scenario by a poor playwright, the morning carefully set aside as my initial four-hour session found me in the veterinarian's office with our two dogs: one with fleas, the other with possible mange — two hours easily subtracted there and then; best laid plans, etc. Tomorrow.

* * *

And now, finally, to a clinical logging of the long haul of preparation. With the first fresh approaches to almost-established repertoire, it becomes apparent to me that little threadbare places must be entirely rewoven and not just doctored up. If it can't be clean, I won't bother at all. No more faking, no more "shmearáge" (Josef's coining).

It is truly a great joy to discover for oneself how great works survive all manner of practice techniques. For example, a movement from Bach is equally valid and beautiful at one-quarter of the indicated tempo. It not only survives but is more than ever therapeutically pacifying and ordering to an over-complex spirit. Beethoven's great moodiness, Chopin's rich chromaticisms, Schumann's nobility; they all survive the rigors of practice — indestructible and, if anything, magnified in the dissection. My notion today is that discounting the pressures of time bearing down, the so-called "work sessions" will be euphemisms for "joy sessions"...licentious, self-indulgent orgies, and I feel deeply comforted by the secret new tenant of the spare room of my inner reserve: the Piano.

* * *

Terror will certainly play an important role in the time ahead, though hopefully, in smallish doses. This morning, when suddenly my hands became derailed from the intricate mechanical systems which link one hand position to the next, in a spot where I never had problems before, projections of seas of anonymous faces flashed before my eyes and put me suddenly "up there," my adrenalin-loaded body coping desperately with the situation. We are taught to reinforce the mechanical end of it with photographic images of the music in the brain, auditory responses to melodic lines, intellectual analysis of the structure, etc. None of these served me in this crisis.

The point is simple: I am not ready yet. I *will* be ready and the systems *will* be engraved soundly by November 9th, my first pre-recital recital: two months before I take the show on the road. Four hours daily, five times a week, twenty hours a week — two hundred hours by November 9th. Any moron should be able to do it by then. But how fast an hour is spent at the keyboard. . . .

* * *

A marvelous insight came to me today at the piano. The Beethoven was going all right technically but it felt lacklustre under my fingers. Suddenly I became aware of something I already knew: Beethoven is the man whose human-ness is most revealed to us through his music. I actually at this moment of recognition, donned his cloak, became *him*, experienced the gaiety, the sadness, the anger. And the music sprang to life. If I can manage this transmigration of my soul, or whatever device it is, under tension, I'll be in good shape.

* * *

Another discovery. I will practice with the lid raised. Why not? The sound is so much more beautiful, and the nuances of the tone add to the inspiration. It's like saving good china only for company. It will never wear out. Why not partake of beautiful things all the time? Why should the sound stay locked inside if *I* can be enjoying it?

The mind is sometimes like a spiteful child. The playing might be going along flawlessly well, when up pops the question: "What if? . . ." "What if this" and "What if that" is a good child's game, but it is the deadly enemy of perfection. The conjecture invariably changes to reality, and one no longer has to ask "What if" because "It did"! Along the same lines, if we had a switch to shut off our sensory organs except as they relate to the music, we'd be better off. Once a scent came wafting past my nostrils during a recital and I suddenly started to wonder, "Is *that* person here?" (an association with the scent) and my concentration started to slip. Rustling programs, coughing, doors slamming, all sorts of distractions have to go utterly unnoticed. . . . Complete absorption, terribly hard for me to achieve because I am especially impressionable and receptive to external effects.

* * *

I am planning to take my pillow with me wherever I play. Lest some think it a security blanket, I will explain graphically that it has conformed itself so exactly to my sitting apparatus and is so precisely the dimensions I need, assuming the seats and keyboards are all standard heights, that I can eliminate another hindrance for myself. It is the curse of the pianist to be the only concert instrumentalist having to adapt instantly to a completely unknown quantity — or quality. The least we can do is have our own pillow.

* * *

Except for an occasional miracle at midnight, by which I mean a sudden spurt of inspiration in the dead of the night which usually materializes into the best sounds I ever produce, my general rule is to stick to the mornings. Whether it has to do with sugar levels or the cumulative cares of the day, around four o'clock in the afternoon is a disaster area. If I feel particularly masochistic and I want the old nervous stomach to start working, I can sit down fagged out in the late afternoon and bank all my hopes on what comes out: nothing will. Good luck to me at eight o'clock on a Monday night.

* * *

One hour and a half on Beethoven alone this morning and I feel beautiful. The slow-motion process uncovered myriad details I had never even noticed before, and I thought I knew the Sonata! I am practicing four out of five times with music, on Josef's advice, (even though it is already committed to memory) for that very reason.

The harder I stare the more the lens focuses in on minutiae and the texture becomes richer and richer. Except for a sudden disappointment when I tried it out prematurely full speed ahead, and shouted a profanity which scared the dogs, the entire package was so positive and progressive that I feel drugged.

* * *

Letting it breathe: one of the signs of mature interpretation. The fabric is porous, and each phrase must be an entity in itself, within the entire concept, relieved by breath on both sides. The word is "control," and it comes with security and peace of mind after preoccupation with technical problems is behind: the great mark of the artist.

One good measure of my nerves and lack of peace of mind is my infernal nose. The moisture, if I may be so gross, is directly proportional to the tension. One is reduced to sniffling, surreptitious side-swiping, glistening, and if things are really bad, a moist keyboard. I am looking for a magic pill which shuts that off without tampering with the metabolism.

* * *

One piles on layers of practice just as the soil and silt are piled on through the various ages of the earth. If we could look at these layers just as we can see the strata exposed in the depths of the Grand Canyon, we would see that at a certain definite point, there is a life line: a moment in time when life was breathed into the music — and it ceased to be "just dots" and began to live.

* * *

Telephone Conversation: (A poor attempt is made here to suggest Josef's rich Russian accent.)

"Hello, Josef? This is Carol."

"Hello dahling."

"Josef, I just spoke to the chairman of the Music Department at Queens College, and the only date available to play in their recital hall, which has an excellent piano and seats about 300 is February 5th, four days before Carnegie."

"So?"

"Won't I be too tired?"

"You don't know anyting vot's going on in the concert vorld — I played every night somevere else in Europe — in the morning the rehearsal, the evening — the concert — everyday!"

"But I'm not used to that!"

"Vot do you tink — you are born on the stage? You *get* used to it!"

"So you think I should accept that date?"

"Absolutely!"

"What if I mess things up, and I only have four days to fix it up?"

"Vot kind of attitude is dot? Vot are you vorried about, the cabbages out there? Instead say, 'I'll play better than Rubinstein,' and maybe you vill!"

"What do I do about all those different pianos? What *is* the trick to adapting oneself instantaneously to a new instrument?"

"It's simple, dahling. You simply sit down, stare at the piano and say, 'Obey me!' "

* * *

Yesterday I played for five hours and my body felt light and exhilarated. This morning after only two hours, I'm dead. The back is starting to ache, the neck doesn't feel as though it can support the head, the wrists, even the calf muscles....I could use a great massage right now.

* * *

I just felt the exact moment when "life" was breathed into one of the most introspective Schumann Etudes -Symphoniques. I'm sure it has very much to do with feeling safe in memory and technique, but it's surely more than that. It has to do with being on the same wave length as the composer, total abandon, and an ability to savor all the succulence of a work. The Schumann is dripping with it.

* * *

Tonight I want to consider the whole question of Beethoven's music, who plays it, and how. It's been suggested to me that I am suicidal to play Beethoven in New York. Why? First of all there's the notion of being sufficiently great and ripe to tackle it; and second, the fact that everyone likes his Beethoven a different way, and you can never please everyone, and, chances are, especially not the guy who's sitting out there with his pencil and paper. Fidelman told me if I'm doing this thing for reviews, forget it. Don't do it. You don't play to one person who may or may not be a "cabbage." You go into it doing your best, you don't stake your ego and your future ego on this guy's whims. You know what you are beforehand and afterwards. Along with this, I feel I must play what I love. And Beethoven is tops for me. I adore him. I write him letters! I wrote Testaments back to him. And it did take me mighty long to allow myself the honor of performing Him. The end product will be my Beethoven. It is valid because it projects what it means to me. And I daresay it will certainly be well within the boundaries of what is acceptable Beethoven out of sheer respect. "Boundaries" because he spans from Classical to Romantic, darts from depression to joviality, shifts from mighty fortissimo to subito pianissimos; and great pianist that he was, he presents us with roguish feats to accomplish, all beautifully written for the hand he understood so well. If the listener were to abandon himself to the music without searching and combing the score for little rules which have been broken, he might find that the finished Sonata will be unmistakably Beethoven, but also mine.

* * *

My sheet music to the Bach Italian Concerto looks like a crazy patchwork quilt. It has more notations than printed matter. Every phrase and indication I discussed with Josef, every well thought out finger he suggested, every transformation from "just dots" to meaningful melodic lines...it's all there. I knew a pianist once, not a serious one as will be obvious from the following, who considered it an embarrassment to have a mark on her music, either a teacher's or her own. On the contrary, I flip with sensual pleasure through these precious pages loaded with wise, scholarly, insightful enrichments to the published edition.

Some of my music (from Mittman's own youth), is flaky with age ("like dry toast" he used to say), smells wonderfully warm, and crumbles away with each page-turn. I have sometimes scribbled in, at the appropriate passage, a quotable quote from Fidelman or Mittman, which either demolished me with laughter or embarrassed me into shaping up during the course of a lesson. When I'm reading that page, sometimes years later, the entire value and pleasure of that lesson comes back to me again. One example: I was playing a slow, introspective Schumann piece for Lully (Mittman), which comes to a huge climax in the middle and then to a quiet close. I dragged out the development of this dramatic rise ad boredom, and the climax was almost aborted and certainly not exciting. With a little twinkle in his eyes, Lully said, "Carol, if one wants to be passionate, one can't take so long!"

* * *

This morning it feels particularly lonely at the piano. It's as though the piano and I are condemned to each other for better or for worse. The phone is deathly silent, my friends being respectfully obedient to the 8 a.m. to 12 noon moratorium. The concentration needs harnessing back to the focal points, and even the dogs, (the little one curled up right on my feet at the pedals), are no comfort.

* * *

All I ask for myself is that somehow, when the showdown comes, I can do my own best work, no more, no less. I have finally gained a consistent flow of confidence (extended even into the supermarket). I believe I can do it without the impediments nerves impose. Now to acquire a device to be able to center in at will. Perhaps the yoga course I am taking will offer something. Awareness of and intelligent use of one's breathing apparatus can be a very important factor, as well as the ability to experience one's center of gravity, attain inner peace, and be impervious to exterior pressures.

* * *

Shall I admit in writing that one of my favorite fantasies these days is the image of The Placard outside of Carnegie, plastered up with my likeness on it, for all the sophisticated 57th Street passersby to see for one long important week? And the ad in the *Times* the Sunday before would be another agreeable notion, if I didn't know how shockingly through-the-nose one pays to place it.

* * *

I found out today exactly how physical all this preparation is. The Schumann Études-Symphoniques is a collection of every conceivable pianistic problem in the book. Each variation presents the hand (which so fascinated and tormented Schumann) with new tricks to accomplish. Not choice, but time and priorities held me from it for two days. The muscular tension as a direct function of the short period of disuse was frighteningly crippling. Obviously this is one piece I'll have to go at every single day unless I want rigor mortis to set in.

* * *

There's something to be learned from even the most unlikely circumstances. My family having convinced me to remove my blinders and get away for three or four days, I find myself in astoundingly beautiful Vermont in peak autumn season. I started out wondering what the hiatus in practicing would do to the momentum, the memory, and the muscles. I no longer have to pass those acid tests: in the living room of this gracious colonial house is a gorgeous old Blüthner, the same vintage as Mittman's on which I took my lessons for over twenty years. These old specimens, past their prime, still have the vestiges of their youth and beauty, waiting to be savored and loved.

My first chord revealed that its pitch was a full tone lower than 440 A; the action uneven, the sound thin, as an old person's voice might be. In spite of these obstacles I laced into the Bach, struggling to adapt to a new "do," and I got through it alive. I found exactly to what extent I depend on my ear and where, God help me, if the piano isn't perfectly tuned my ear could let me down. The old piano lent its ripe delicious personality to everything I tried on it. I now look forward to what each individual instrument has to offer me and, through me, to the music. One can have a love affair with each new instrument and never have it come between one's self and one's own dear piano at all.

After that session I had noticeable muscle tension, and I wondered why, since the old action was flabby with age. It then came to me that I was sitting differently (on the old piano stool), higher than at home, and that the angle of my arm was at a steeper incline to the keyboard, putting strain on new muscles. I must make sure I am sitting at exactly the same height at all times.

* * *

The Chopin Third Impromptu is eluding my memory like quicksilver. This little pearl of a piece, not often played, a fresh, spontaneous, dreamy thing, would be just right for the program. It's a short interlude and it suits me, which I think is important. But what perversity does it contain that it resists my memorizing the middle section? It's this very elusiveness, ironically, which is the charm of the piece. Do I dare perform it with the music? Why is it that all other instrumentalists, including harpsichordists blithely give their recitals undaunted by any stigma attached to their use of music on the stage, and the pianist has yet another handicap added to the fact that he plays a strange instrument, that fear of memory loss. I may brave the storms of criticism and sneak that page out there, or I may sadly have to give that dear Impromptu up, which I would sorely hate to do.

* * *

I am grateful for something that happened today. My parents asked me to play part of the program for them, a sort of command performance thing. I wasn't thrilled at the prospect of tackling my pieces on their old Knabe, but what-the-devil, I sat down and a wonderful thing occurred to me not far into the Beethoven: the very differences which have been so frightening to me in terms of instant adjustments to other pianos actually add to the mystery and serve as a distraction. It is the unknown quality of each individual instrument which can be surprisingly refreshing and unique, and which can offer some especially new and varied gift to the composition...in much the same way as a sculptor allows a chunk of stone to suggest itself to him. If an old has-been piano can make me aware of its little ripenesses, imagine what the presumably fine, well-kept one I will be using, may have to offer. Today's episode reminded me of the passage in Romain Rolland's *Jean-Christophe* in which an old professor, whose ancient piano has just been passed off as having seen better days, presses two wonderfully resonant notes and says, "Yes, but see, it still has beautiful eyes!" Which brings us to the notion that a vanity exists between the pianist and his instrument, even if it's "a child only a mother could love."

The great black mass that is my piano has immense beauty to me. All that potential, standing stodgily on three strategic legs and capable of the widest reaches and varieties of sound of any instrument in the world. I once realized that I am so vain about my piano that I would sooner hear a compliment about its virtues than mine.

* * *

After I had played the complete Bach for Josef one day, he said, "Bravo, that was beautiful! All the details were there." A supreme compliment coming from him, but I was not satisfied. "Why does it feel so tentative? Why do I always feel perched on the narrow margin of disaster with it?" He told me that he never played it through without that feeling, and that it is so chock full of responsibilities to the minutiae that one can never let down one's guard. (Had I known that, I might not have chosen it for *the* program, no matter how I love it.) To feel always on the brink between perfection and disaster will not contribute to my ultimate peace of mind. It boils down to human frailty. A machine could produce the exact results each time, of course, but it's the delicate and varied shadings that reflect fleeting states of mind and add that slightly impromptu quality to the solid, basic, worked-out mass of the work. I will have to accept the tenuous feelings as part of the entire package.

A friend's suggestion to think about where you are in the music and not where you are going, is a good way of trying to avoid a mishap; in Bach, above all else, it is most difficult to wiggle out of a problem, as anyone who has fugued frantically around the "circle of fifths" knows all too well.

* * *

Yesterday morning's four-hour session was a wanton orgy of a different order from beginning to end. It started with a great cup of coffee, went through two T.V. talk shows, one crossword puzzle, some letter-writing, and some more coffee. I simply decided not this morning. It was not without a measure of guilt and trepidation that I sacrificed the precious parcel of time to the utterly mundane.

On the other hand, today I got a start at 7:30 A.M. and by 9:00, after some super-intense work, was aware of a strong physical tax on my body. I heard Rubinstein once say that if a pianist expressed the same arm and finger actions on a table instead of a keyboard, there would be an amazing demonstration of the physicality of the labor. Without the distraction of the auditory end of it the sheer exercise is startlingly visible.

Everyone knows about the power of positive think-ing, but unless I have a prescription or a recipe for a thought process, my thoughts run rampant, usually to-ward the fearsome aspects, and are tricky to control. A friend, who is giving me a smattering of what Yoga has to offer, from mental relaxation to physical rejuvenation, introduced me to a concept of Affirmation — a conscious reiteration of concrete notions such as "I can do it," "I am doing it," "I have done it," as well as mental images of the act of performing my best and receiving acclamatory reactions. Incorporated here and there into my daily routine, I begin to be convinced that there is no other alternative but to succeed, and the feelings of imminent success and accomplishment as well as confidence have crept into my veins, purging and flushing out most of the anxiety.

* * *

How I love to make music! Most often the joy is too much to contain and the syndrome of "the tree falling in the forest with no one there to hear the noise" (Is there, then, truly, a noise?) preys on me. At those times the urge to pick up the phone and dial-a-friend, many of whom have expressed a sincere desire to sit in on a practice session, takes over. Naturally there is no such thing as practicing with someone around. That's called showing off, but it's a necessary and valuable part of the whole creative process, understandable only to those with the same needs. I once had an acquaintance who accused me of only being happy to play for others, and being unable to find pleasure in it for myself alone. I tried to clarify the nature of those needs by likening it to a writer's frustration at having a book lying unread on a shelf, and the incompleteness of the creative process without that last crucial reception phase. This morning, however, I had one of my rare fulfillments of being myself enough to play for, (with only faint rumblings deep within of needing to share it).

* * *

Someone told me that a famous violinist, when asked what his thoughts were while he was deeply involved in a virtuoso display in performance answered, "If it's a Saturday night, chances are I'm thinking about the bagels and lox I'll be having for breakfast the next morning." So he admits he abandons himself to a sort of rote which carries him through safely to the end. In fact it works. I had noticed before I ever heard this anecdote that some of my own best playing was done while my mind was wandering like a gypsy. Sometimes I cannot, for the life of me, harness those brain waves to the focal point. Other times, almost as a result of over-concentration and zealousness, disaster strikes. How to handle a performance? I don't think we have a choice. The currents in the air, and the dynamics of each separate situation dictate our state of mind.

* * *

After it's all over, I am going to treat myself to a spanking new edition of the Beethoven Sonatas as a reward. It will be the Tovey *Urtext*. The way I see it, nine out of ten editors have no better basic instincts than

I do, so why shouldn't I trust my own readings of Beethoven's meticulous markings? When I compared my own old edition to the Urtext, I found it shocking how much non-Beethoven we accept as the spoken word. It is so purifying to strip down to the naked score and start fresh with that, adding only the slightest discreet personal touches. Why blindly adopt someone else's feelings? The copy looks sterile and austere by comparison to the heavily-laden edited ones, but there is grandeur and stark awesomeness in knowing that every note and indication is pure and valid.

* * *

I went to Fidelman's today expecting to zip through everything uninterrupted and totally admired. I should have known better. There is no such thing as perfection and the goals one can strive for are infinite. I now know that is one of the marks of a great teacher: to extend the reaches even wider than before.

Josef and I locked horns at one point on an interpretive idea in the Schumann. We were in a deadlock of strong temperaments, so I said, half-joking, half-angry, "Whose concert is this anyway, yours or mine?" Josef calmly returned, "Schumann's."

In fact the lessons are rich with wit and we have a great time. After I played the middle movement of the Beethoven, Josef said in complete deadpan, "You'd better rent the hall for two evenings, Carol." Innocently, I asked "Why?", setting him up for, "If you're going to play *that* slowly, it will take until the second night to finish it." Another shot: "Don't pretend you are playing all the notes. When people are paying, they want to hear every note!"

* * *

I am finally having a wonderful time with the Schumann. When I got over the "Études" and into the "Symphoniques" stage, I had a full palette of colors in hand to paint from and tools with which to orchestrate the full gamut of human emotions.

The Finale is one of the most technically difficult pieces in the entire work, and yet it is a game. As long as the technique is bothersome, there cannot be the complete abandon that must be the modus operandi. The folks who march right through it in perfect time are missing the boat. It has built-in triumphs and wild spontaneity, and must be played with wit, and ego — even though it is repetitious. There are dozens of ways to keep it interesting: sudden drops in volume, strettos, crescendos, texture changes, and each time the gala theme re-enters, a shameless display of enthusiasm without fear of being vulgar.

Schumann wrote five "Anhangen" (literally hangings-on or appendices) after completing the Symphonic Etudes. They are all lovely, but I find the entire work too lengthy when all are performed. The piece is generally played either with or without them, and I have heard them incorporated in several ways into the main body of the work, preserving the Finale, of course, for the end. I have decided to play only my two favorites, Variations I and V, although I've never heard that done. Josef and I poured through texts to find if there was any indication from Schumann himself, or any precedent as to where to place these wonderful bonuses in performance. Apparently there is no rule, so I am putting them between the last Etude and the Finale. It works very well harmonically, and the contrast between the exquisite fifth Anhang and the Finale is very dramatic.

The fifth Anhang has been subtitled "The Birdie's Funeral" by my friends who know the following little story. Several years ago when I had first begun to read the Schumann, I was so enchanted by this Variation (and still am) that I must have played it twenty times on end in one session. Kim, our fine young flutist, who was much littler then, quietly came and left a note on the piano while I was playing, and disappeared. When I stopped to look at it, I read the following rhapsody: "O Mommy, that piece is so beautiful! And you are so beautiful, I love you! It sounds like birdies having a funeral. Love, Kim." This, complete with a sketch of a bevy of tearful birds around a bird-sized coffin. This was a more-than-precious tribute, and it has been permanently taped into my music as an inspiration to me.

* * *

I have a good feeling that a week from now I shall play my best at the first recital. After three exuberant practice-sessions on that beautiful piano in its most resonant hall, I was refreshed by inspiration offered by these new tools. My prime concern reaches beyond this date though, and into the three months to go before Carnegie: how *will* I keep it fresh? Josef recently made me laugh when he recalled a Hungarian girl who lived in his building, leaving with a suitcase. When he asked her where she was going, she answered, "To Paris, for inspiration." In Josef's opinion, one does not "go to Paris," or Timbuktu for inspiration; it is right there in the music. My lovely old piano has given me all it has to offer, and we and the music, like a ménage-à-trois, know each other almost too well.

I'll have to continue with the watch-guard tactics, practicing at a slow tempo to make sure that no mistakes creep in; and I think I will save performances for special listeners, and only when special insights come to me — much the same way as a singer will rehearse in falsetto, or undersing and save the full-throated sound for the performance. Otherwise, I fear I will deflower the music and begin to sound stale.

Probably a day or two off, here and there, will not hurt either and because there is a joint recital with Dennis (cello and piano) coming up, as well as a few commitments in the Spring, by now I can afford to divide my time and slowly start digging into some new stuff. There shouldn't be any interference technically at this point.

* * *

It isn't a good idea to let your mind wander and become aware of various persons in the audience; one person likes his performance nice and schmaltzy, another is a super-conservative purist who likes his Bach only on the harpsichord; another doesn't mind a certain amount of *laissez-aller* in favor of the complete line and meaning; another chalks off the entire performance on the basis of two wrong notes. Some look for outward evidence of expressiveness — facial responses or body language, others resent anything but a stony countenance as a distraction. And no matter how special or sympathetic in tastes or opinions any one listener may be, in the end you have only yourself — to express and to please.

*   *   *

There will be seven persons in the audience who form a rarified body of support: our Piano Workshop Group. We are eight pianists who have happened upon a rather unique formula of special value to us all. A quite informal and heterogeneous bunch — stylistically, culturally and tempermentally — we are, however, entirely compatible. The monthly meetings serve as a forum where we can try out new pieces and impose tensions on ourselves which simulate those of public performance: after all, what more fearsome audience than a solid bloc of pianists each of whom knows every note being played? These opportunities have been priceless for me the past couple of months.

Over the years, we have become such good friends, that we often have to consciously curb our impulses to share the extra-musical events in our lives and get down to business. Each member prepares a work almost every time; this is followed by a constructive talk-session ranging from the more ephemeral matters of interpretation to particular problems like fingering. Very often a pianist will repeat a "performance" either in the same session, if there is time, or the following month. Thus, not only are we privy to the metamorphoses in each other, but often a single work might be passed from hand to hand as we each take a crack at it. The dynamics of individuation are simply fascinating.

But the most wonderful aspect of the group is surely the genuine interest and concern for each other's pianistic development. We have been meeting for about ten years, and each of us has grown considerably in that time. Some have had active careers years ago and have settled into more domestic existences, others have put off, until recently, plans to go public. Present, en masse, at all recitals, we keep each other on our toes, and the extra moral support (and I daresay, vicarious nerves) will be gratefully felt at a certain "happening."

* * *

Today, four days before my first recital in the series, I'm having a good case of why I haven't chosen to do more playing in public. In spite of the fact that the program went smoothly for Josef a couple of days ago, and in spite of all the positive thinking, I am being plagued by the all too familiar signs of nervous tension: stomach unrest, a lump in the throat, hallucinations of musical disasters, self-scrutiny, the works. One gorgeous package.

What I think it is that creates this precarious state is a keen sense of responsibility and a certain ethic: to the listener from the composer. I am simply the middle-man and on my shoulders rest what I consider more serious than joyful — the faithful transformations of the dots on the page into messages meant to be conveyed to the world. The joy can come later with the achievement.

One hour later. With uncanny timing a pianist friend referred me to a quote in the *Times* today of Rostropovich chiding a student: "You play as though you've been condemned. Don't take it too serious or too hard. It should be like singing to yourself."

Another close friend gave me an "order" to drop those "ponderous notions" (the middle-man concept, communicating the message, etc.) and have some fun. In her view the most important tribute to the composers, (and an end in itself) is that I love their music, and my creative act of performance should be a source of pleasure and satisfaction.

I told Josef about my middle-man notion, and he said, "The five-and-ten-cent musicians are middle-men but *you* are a *personality* — an extension of the composer — his representative, and as such, you must improvise! And that's where all the fun comes in."

Today's consensus seems to be that I had better start enjoying more and worrying less.

* * *

Encore Pieces and How to Choose Them. Obviously one does not want to break one's neck after the mammoth efforts of an entire program, but neither should it be anti-climactic. I think it is a good idea to have several up one's sleeve and see which one suits the needs and moods of the moment. It may be that I will be crippled with muscle cramps and dead tired, in which case a sweet little soothing nocturne would do the trick; or, if I have adequate energy in reserve, a spritely, capricious little number (such as "Chicks" from Mussorgsky's "Pictures at an Exhibition") is a provocative way to leave the hall. All assuming one will be asked for any at all!

* * *

Bothersome details keep cropping up to obliterate the main issue. 1. The pedals are rendered too high to use because the piano has been put up on casters for easy handling. This is finally overcome by a thick piece of lumber being dragged from the lumber yard over to the Recital Hall and placed underneath — extending from the seat to the pedals, in effect raising the "floor" to meet the pedals. 2. The publicity is late, allowing people only a couple of days notice before the concert. Demoralizing visions of playing to an empty hall. 3. The search for a suitable nasal-drying drug is as yet fruitless due to the fatiguing effects of the anti-histamines.

Two days before the recital, and still trying to keep the "joy" in mind, obliterating the stress, I remind myself of a factory inspector holding up a textile to the light for scrutiny to see imperfections in the weave. Suddenly out of the blue, in the Bach I become aware that even though it seems to "go" by itself, there are phrases which I don't quite "know backwards." As there is no such thing as being overprepared, two hours of slow Bach are put on the agenda.

It is a fascinating mental phenomenon that when I am relaxed, immediately my train of thought goes off on a stream of semi-consciousness of its own, and the music sounds relaxed, having been put on "automatic pilot" (the bagels and lox syndrome); but the minute stress is introduced, and the mind is completely involved with the intricacies of the music; that's where the trouble starts. And all this is not under one's control. If I wanted to *will* my mind to wander in the interests of safety, I couldn't.

* * *

Never again will I be so confident as to leave my music home on recital day. Once, a couple of years ago, in an intermission after a successful first half, I was anticipating the Ravel "Alborada del Grazioso" and fingering it on the table backstage. Suddenly, after the four-measure introduction of Spanish rhythmic figures,

I drew a blank! So I tried it again. Nothing. Meanwhile, the lights had gone out and I, having no music to refer to for a quick visual photograph of the bridge measure in question, had no choice but to march out blindly with a desperate prayer that God would save me. I began the piece and could not get into the fifth measure, but without breaking the rhythm, in one of the most adrenalin-charged moments of my life, repeated the four-measure intro in perfect time. The *third* set of those four bars flowed miraculously into the rest of the piece. Only pianists who knew the work were aware of the crisis; the rest of the audience must have thought, "That's a rather long introductory passage!" The next day (after I had related the incident), Mittman yelled, "Idiot! Don't you know *never* to play on the table?" His mock rage was always tempered with tenderness and he frequently name-called: "Rascal!" he would say if I found a deceptive fingering which enabled me to achieve some pianistic feat which he thought would stump me; "Little gypsy!" if I got too schmaltzy.

* * *

I spoke to Josef tonight on the phone and he asked me how I feel. I told him the playing was fine, but that I didn't care much for the feeling in my stomach. There was a short silence (perhaps a reflection of his disapproval of my dwelling on that), and then, "Carol, you're not playing with your stomach, you're playing with your fingers."

* * *

One day before the recital and I never expected to feel so free and relaxed as I do. I know now that there is no way to analyze it, or to determine how I'll feel at any given time. It would be so wonderful to sail right into tomorrow at 2:15 p.m. with the same blithe spirit that is in me now. What a mystery our bodies and minds are!

* * *

Impressions In a Backstage Closet:

The facilities leave something to be desired. I find myself at 2:10 p.m. in a no-exit 7' x 5' sterile chamber with cement block walls, three chairs, a pitcher of water, my music, and a crossword puzzle. Beyond the wall there is the increasing murmur of the audience filling the seats in the room. I expect, momentarily, a short buzzer to signal that the lights have been dimmed and my appearance on the stage is being awaited. Two-thirty and no signal. My hands are alternately perspiring and cold to the touch. My stomach is churning to beat the band, and no matter how hard I "meditate," with due respects to all the Yogi, or concentrate on the crossword puzzle, the good old nerves are in full bloom.

Then, ten insufferably eternal minutes later, the piercing buzz startles me and I find myself entering, smiling confidently, and seating myself at the keyboard.

* * *

With superhuman effort, I narrowly escaped disaster several times in the first movement of the Bach Italian Concerto. It simply cannot be done to the best of one's ability with shaking hands, and although I came through it alive and even well, I have decided there must be a better way to start the program. The solution came later. To everything else, having calmed down sufficiently, I was able to give my best, and it was almost a pure joy to be up there producing. The response was terrific and I felt a certain measure of triumph, although the disturbing issue of the Bach was underlying all my positive experiences.

When it finally dawned on me to replace the Italian Concerto with my beloved Partita I in B♭ by Bach, it was as though a great weight was lifted from me. Here is a work which I played several years ago with success and ardor under the tensions of a public performance — in short, a composition equally great and complex, the same length, same composer, same everything, but chemically suited to me far better than the other. The precariousness and consequent fear were washed away by that decision, and the reviving of an old love has now become a delightful chore. I have always felt that the Partita must have been written especially for *me,* something I never could have said about "the Italian." It's the right way to feel about a piece and makes a ton of sense to use it on such an important program. I cannot play the opening Praeludium without savoring its delicate ornaments and being carried along by its gentle, mellifluous theme. A far cry from being studiously preoccupied with details and feeling as though one is being judged for scholarly execution of the minutiae. The former pacifies and soothes, the latter magnifies the tension. (If the Partita resists revival and doesn't come through to save this spot on the program, it will be as though a good friend is deserting me. Every time I get snagged in it, I ask myself, "Shall I try the Italian again?". . . .)

* * *

Except for the novelty of working on the Partita, getting myself back to practicing the rest of the program is nearly impossible. The feeling of it all being behind — the aftermath of a recital — is stronger than the awareness of the reality of the four to come. Rationally I *know* I had better keep practicing consistently and persistently up to and through all the recitals, but the body and mind definitely need a rest, and the battery needs recharging. The easiest approach is purely mechanical workouts, devoid of inspirational elements. After all, it *is* a job!

* * *

I have caught myself snickering superciliously at the silliness of compliments given to me by non-musicians regarding the "tremendous feat of memory" involved in a recital program. Very much taken for granted, it is part-of-the-parcel and I have never given it much thought when it went smoothly, only annoyance when I ran into snags. The truth is, however, that it is not silly; and suddenly I have a tremendous desire to understand the highly complex system of impulses and such which figure into it. It is similar to my occasional urges to open up one of those pocket-sized sophisticated computers to see the terminals and networks of programming so neatly compacted into its container. Obviously nothing would be revealed to me therein; it would remain one of the Unfathomable Mysteries, and so is the Memory. My pieces are now programmed inside me physiologically, neurologically, intellectually, emotionally, and if some day soon I feed it a new batch of "data," the old by-ways of programmed responses would yield to the new.

Actually, the memorizing is often a royal pain, and I sometimes come to wonder if senility isn't setting in at the ripe old age of thirty-six. Mittman once said to me, "You want to memorize this? Then suffer!" By which he meant that it is often a long, tiresome process. "It" doesn't just happen. The thing has to "be committed" to memory.

With me, memory has admittedly been based largely on ear, although perfect pitch is not always a dependable crutch in emergencies. In fact I think it is sometimes a detriment, especially if one begins to depend on the ear to the exclusion of other faculties in the process of memorization. By endless repetition the sound becomes second nature, and the ear guides the hand through the appropriate motions. With others whom I know, it is a predominantly visual process as the page is photographed, and they are, in effect "reading" the music.

In some extremely obstinate and resistant passages one has to resort to mnemonic tricks and gimmicks to cajole the memory into cooperating. I have two such places: one in the Schumann, the other in the Beethoven. I concocted for myself, some nonsense acronyms made up of the letters of the stubborn notes, which solved the problem, except for the distraction of having such drivel appear suddenly in the midst of the most profound passages. It is with a measure of embarrassment that I admit to the existence of these devices at all; but, it works.

My piano is situated in the living room in such a way that I can look out to a most peaceful vista of woodlands. All day long my feathered friends come to the feeder, also in view from the piano; and the sunlight filters through the leaves of the hanging plants at the window. These combined images are all together in one "coup d'oeil" and are so visually nourishing to me, that in a sort of photosynthetic process of my own, I transform this "energy" into music-making. I can actually feel the synthesis taking place within me. The result is what George Moore, the English novelist, described as "audible color and visible sound" in this harmonious fusion of the senses.

* * *

I think I have undergone some severe personality changes through this somewhat ascetic life-style I have created for myself. I had wondered to what extent I could unhinge myself from the need to communicate, and the time-consuming habits of close friendships. To a certain extent my writing down (on the pad which is always at the piano) of an occasional thought, has replaced human contact. But I have to somehow acknowledge with a certain reluctance, that our dogs have played an important role. For comic relief from a monastic few hours of "devotion," I have recently taken to saying something aloud to them, and judging from their cocked heads and limpid eyes, I would swear they understand. I wouldn't be surprised if they were to be equipped with fingers instead of paws, that they might, through osmosis, have learned my program, and be able to do it themselves! Certainly they have learned some of the music for, amazingly, they recognize closing bars and codas, and anticipate the respite and the playtime several bars before the end. They also suddenly become respectfully silent (and resigned?) when I set to the task around 8 a.m., understanding quite well that I want no distractions. Our New York audiences could learn a thing or two from them.

* * *

I find myself sandwiched between two critics and I'd like to sic them on each other in this instance. I started working on a Chopin Waltz, a little played, elegant one (in D-flat, opus posthumous), which I have taught and adored yet never performed. It was a labor of love to memorize and get it in shape for an encore piece. My husband, a fan of the vintage recordings of Kreisler, McCormack, etc., showed up on the scene and suggested I "take more time" with each phrase and then proceeded to dissect and analyze the waltz, bit by bit and prescribe what he felt the style should be. Much of what he offered was valid and appealing, and so I docilely adopted the ideas and integrated them into the waltz. The next day Josef said, "You are playing the piece like an old maid." He expounded on the importance of understatement, and stressed how one must not over-romanticize Chopin, who built enough emotion right into the music. We talked about finesse and touch, and tempo and tone; and I docilely began to adopt *his* ideas in to the waltz. Surely I am artist enough to turn a waltz into a thing of loveliness by myself! I have half a mind to get up at the end of the recital and say, "Josef Fidelman will now play the right hand, and Guy Parker will now do the left hand of the Chopin Waltz in D-flat."

* * *

Sitting in the audience at a piano concert of one of the "greats," two weeks before giving a recital of one's own is a mixed bag. On the plus side, there's the joy of the music and the sharing of the public display vicariously. I have moments of unbridled eagerness to be the one "up there" partaking. But the minuses are considerable too. In moments of technical difficulty, only another pianist can really empathize with the performer. Suddenly the entire situation becomes un-enviable.

* * *

Whether or not anyone will ever read these pages, their value to me as a catharsis, as a focal point for surplus nervous and creative energies, and as a sort of self-analysis, is still considerable. And so, not so much to be read, but as an exposé of myself to myself, I have to admit the following: it is not easy for me to take criticism amiably and generously, no matter how delicately it is given. (I do not include "lesson" situations wherein I am there expressly for that purpose). It refers to those who are close to me, and is probably a function of the pressure of time (left before a recital) as well as the fear of undoing established patterns, safely engraved in my hands by now.

Admittedly, it is a form of paranoia and an outward manifestation of insecurity. Because the piano has become an extension of myself, I suppose the criticism is felt as an attack upon my person.

And yet it is a strange anomaly that although the piano playing is a part of me, and I am unable to imagine myself without its being a major portion of my identity, I want to be "whole" to others without it.

*   *   *

Somebody told me that a pianist of some renown, who was at the hall at which I will present my second pre-recital, saw my program and asked, "Who is this Carol Montparker?" Then he added, "Either she is crazy to attempt such a program, or she is terrific. I wouldn't miss this on a bet!" Now I knew that my program was no mere child's play, but it made me wonder which of the two alternatives was true if, indeed, there was any validity to the statement at all. The incident was a boat-rocker any way I chose to interpret it.

*   *   *

What are the ingredients of a nervous breakdown? You take a cupful of mis-scheduling, just enough so that the precious two hours of orientation on an unfamiliar piano are wiped off an already crammed schedule. Add a dash of stress upon finding the room unbelievably unesthetic and dead acoustically. Last, a pound of panic thrown into the pot from the first touch on the instrument which reveals it to be stiff and unyielding in action, and brittle in tone.

Josef advises me to simply consider it a rehearsal on a bad piano, and a good friend who seems to know what to say at the right time recalled to me that Rubinstein, when confronted with an inferior instrument, shrugged philosophically and said, "So, I shall make this piano sound better than it ever has before."

In fact when one has distractions other than one's own proficiency, things are likely to go better. At one of my most important concerts, a solo appearance with an orchestra in the Brahms D minor Concerto, I was actually quite ill, having had a stomach virus all week, with fever up to the very moment of the performance. I was so concerned lest I become ill on the stage that the playing went by itself. Now that I am remembering, in another instance, the piano was so poor that my preoccupation with overcoming its flaws took my mind off the usual sources of tension.

I have already benefited in two ways from the prospect of performing on this mediocre piano: it doesn't have as rich a treble as its bass, in fact it is a struggle to get rich tones out in particularly demanding passages in the higher registers, the most serious case being the last chord in the Schumann, the climax of this epic work. So I sat down and pondered the chord and lo! I saw an easier division of labor between the right and left hands that had never occurred to me before, which will be less of a risk, and which will produce a fuller sounding Finale on any piano.

The second insight was also born of necessity: in order to get a sweet pianissimo on this unsubtle instrument, I was forced into trying a technique which I had hitherto avoided: playing the two left pedals simultaneously with my left foot (the una corda and the sostenuto) while using the right foot on the damper. Suffice it to say that it will be a useful technique in future work as well.

*　*　*

I was looking idly at my hands for a long time today, and I find I like them. They would never appeal to anyone by the usual standards of feminine contours or embellishment, and I am often self-consciously aware of them at a dinner table. They are not slim, graceful hands with tapered manicured nails, lily white and smooth. They are strong, developed, working hands which in some way always seem to have on them a hint of whatever I am involved in. In the Springtime there is the roughness from working the soil; during periods when I am painting there are signs of the more permanent pigments, so hard to remove from the pores; and in this, The Year of the Piano, my hands are quite visibly changed: networks of muscles, bones and veins are close to the surface, and the components of the machinery can be seen clearly through the thin skin holding it all together. The nails are exactly to the ends of the fingers, and the fingers' ends are somewhat blunted with the slightest indications of calluses. The element of ivory (or its synthetics) is no more foreign to them than the air itself.

*　*　*

As I approach this next recital I have a highly droll view of the whole thing. I see the situation as rather humorous: my beating my guts out on a stiff piano in an ugly room, expending twice the normal effort in order to come out even. Obviously one cannot get up in front of an audience and give a song and dance such as: "Folks, I just wanted to tell you that the action on this piano is three times stiffer than my own...also notice that the tone is uniformly harsh. This is the timbre of the instrument itself and not my own characteristic sound. Also...etc." If I were not so aware of a certain hostile listener who "is not going to miss this on a bet," I might even consider walking out and saying something like "Any requests?" or "Step right up folks, the act is about to begin." As idiotic as this all sounds, I welcome it as a healthy relief from the oppressively heavy tension which usually grips me around this time.

* * *

On the phone with Josef, I mentioned that I hadn't touched the piano at all today, and he tried to impress me with the importance of the "daily routine," although I was not in an impressible mood. I said I always feel twice as refreshed the next day after being away from it, and with slight sarcasm he returned, "No dahling, it's not 'refreshed,' it's 'surprised.' "

Many of Josef's expressions were in German or Russian, losing something in translation. "Hals und bein-bruch," for example, is somehow more fun to hear backstage before a recital than "Break a leg," even though it translates to an even grizzlier malediction: (Break your neck and bones!)

* * *

My program would be characterized as a traditional, orthodox one with the possible exception that I have not paid the traditional lip service to the contemporary scene. Nor, have I juggled the order around "creatively" in an effort to appear to have hidden profound insights, or scholarly, intellectual rationales as to why Bach would be more valid or fresh as a concluding work. I will play, chronologically, Bach, Beethoven, Schumann and Chopin — to me, an entirely satisfying progression.

We attended a recent recital in which the soloist gave an entirely atonal program which, even to us, as serious musicians, sounded like one run-on string of dissonances. He got a rave review, with nary a word such as, "Yes, but someday we'd like to hear him play Mozart." In fact there was a recent scandal in which a reviewer was revealed to have based his ravings on pure "whim," with no actual knowledge of the modern works in question at all. One wonders what the point of playing in public is. Presumably, communication ought to figure into it, and if 90% of the listeners are "out of it," unless the artist is completely committed to the genre, or is out to dupe the critics, what would be the point? There are obviously no more rules. One is increasingly being presented with All-Bach or All-Brahms, as well as All-Contemporary, so it must be assumed that criticisms can no longer be based on program selection.

* * *

Ideally, the recital should be an artistic experience unfettered by gimmickry. Love ought to be the determining factor, so that the artist, as well as the audience, gets the full measure of joy from the experience. That's what I am trying to do.

* * *

Why me, now? I think before we know it, we pass from a stage of life consisting of *doing,* into a phase largely based on *reflecting.* It would have been easy to continue to say to myself, and to others, I could have done it. But the loose strands of unfinished business, indeed the unrealized dreams, would no doubt have haunted me to the end of my days.

This summer I was somehow, suddenly, in better shape, pianistically, than ever before. I found myself voraciously devouring and desperately seeking bits of opportunities to play and receive confirmation of my underlying notion of, "if not now, when?"

I didn't realize how precariously close to the decision I must have been teetering, until an off-hand conjecture from a dear friend triggered the gears into motion; and before I knew it, I was actually invaded and taken over by a force propelling me efficiently through the necessary arrangements, while I stood watching the phenomenon as a slightly awed spectator. Thus, here I am.

* * *

This evening I made believe that there was no program scheduled in four nights' time, and I licentiously leafed through the music cabinet, lingering lovingly on all my hundreds of neglected, beloved pieces for which there has been no time at all these last months. And, I experienced regret: for each wonderful work which I feel close to, and could not include on the program. The most pronounced lump in my throat came from Brahms. How could I have omitted him from this important recital? So, almost as an atonement for what felt like betrayal, I spieled through Rhapsodies, Intermezzi, and Capriccios, and how intoxicating it was to experience the old glorious sonorities under my fingers. I realized afterwards, that the most gorgeous fantasy I could conjure up would be to keep that audience there, captive, (better still, captivated) into the wee hours, and drag out every last morsel of music that I would have wanted to play, until I dropped with fatigue, but I don't think I would. It would be a sort of ecstatic perpetual motion, and they'd have to drag me away.

* * *

Today I went back to the recital hall and had a private conference with the piano in question, and we settled a few items between the two of us. Josef is right: you can talk to a piano.

* * *

When we bought me this beautiful old Steinway (which I consider myself lucky to have found) about eight years ago, the delivery day was one of the most exciting in my life. How long I had waited to have a responsive, wonderful instrument of my own. At first I stared at the imposing sight for hours on end with occasional urges to make sacrificial offerings to it, and then came a run-on déluge of bits and pieces that I couldn't wait to try out on it. . . fickle bursts of inspiration shifting from one work to another. It took me weeks to settle into any serious business, and I guarded, jealously, the privilege of touching the instrument.

Along with these musical fancies there were others, much more mundane. With its quasi-formal concert-ebony finish, it was the most imposing piece of furniture in the room; and I inaugurated all sorts of insane little rules and regulations about what might or might not be placed upon it. I found out from experts how I might best preserve the finish, and I became compulsive about squaring away the music currently in use into neat piles.

The piano is a model "A" built in the 1920's, the "Golden Age of Steinways," and my respect for the piano has, if anything, increased over the years because of its singularly pure and evocative resonance and tone, compared to the dozens of good instruments I've played since. But when I look at it standing there today, I almost have to laugh out loud. I have at least six stacks — somewhat less than squared away — of varying significances that only I can fathom. There's the recital music itself in several editions, but then there is a conglomeration of prospective encore material; there's a pile of ensemble work — for flute, cello or violin and piano, with which I am always involved to one extent or another. Then there is a pile of my scribblings: this chronicle on pads, typed portions in folders, all reflections relating to my musical routine. Then there are manila envelopes with the paraphernalia which is accumulating from the New York recital and others: contracts, correspondence, photos and proofs, typed programs, printed ones, flyers, newspaper clippings. In short, that corner of the room, (there's a piano somewhere under all of it) has become my office, and the beehive activity has precluded all my considerations of the aesthetics of the decor.

* * *

The over-quoted and unpleasant saying "Misery loves company" is all too true, I think. While listening to a pianist-host of a musical talk-show on WNCN radio this morning, I heard him refer to his own debilitating nervous tensions and then of Horowitz'. First came an overwhelming urge to giggle (my "banana-peel" sense of humor) and then a realization of what good company I am in, in these backstage chambers with cold clammy hands and restive stomachs.

On the same program afterwards, they played a lovely old recording of my great teacher Fidelman's great teacher, Heinrich Neuhaus (whose pupils included besides Josef Fidelman, Gilels, Richter, Lupu, and many of the most renowned Russian pianists.) I had a deep gut reaction of overwhelming pride in the lineage and heritage which has been imparted to me. Leopold Mittman, who was also my great teacher imbued me with his inheritance handed down from the great Polish teacher, Alexander Michailowski, and my years with him were not confined to a study of the piano, but were like a marathon course in the Humanities. I absorbed like a thirsty sponge anecdotes of experiences from his artist's life in the culturally turbulent and exciting meccas like pre-war Paris and Berlin, and much of my art education was gathered in Lully's garret-like studio, where his old Blüthner as well as hundreds of books, paintings and photos created an old-world atmosphere which was wonderfully conducive to making beautiful music.

* * *

It might help to analyze why I was somewhat disappointed in last night's recital (pre-recital #2) instead of accepting resignedly the fact that the impediments I knew would be present, were, and just leaving it at that. I would be deluding myself to accept this rationalization. I know, too well, that a professional must be able to play under any adverse condition, so analyze I must.

To begin, my disappointments were relative to my own potential: no disasters struck, and the adrenalin and pitch got me through potentially embarrassing moments by the skin of my teeth. In fact if I ever thanked God for my ear it would be last night when photographs of the written passages in question faded from my mind's eye and I had to re-compose the tune and re-construct the chords as I thought the composer would have intended (audacious!), these for the deceptively interminable length of a single bar.

The Partita agreed with me chemically, much more than the Italian Concerto. But let's face it — any Bach is fragile, tenuous and so pure that the slightest flaw is magnified a hundred-fold. When the artist is so vulnerable, he should ideally be placed in a soundproof booth. No wonder Glenn Gould has chosen to keep his superb Bach from the rigors of public performance in favor of recording. No matter how minute the imperfection, it is that which lingers on to haunt and harass, obliterating all the good stuff.

I was actually pleased with the Beethoven except for occasionally unavoidable imbalances in tonal control due to the alien action of that particular piano.

The Schumann is apparently going to be my *tour de force*. It is obviously, (knock wood!) a reliably consistent success for which I should be grateful and maybe even a bit proud. It seems to be "playing me" at this stage.

The Chopin which was my best piece in the last recital, gave me the biggest headache in this one. How to account for that? It may be as simple as the fact that I was tremendously drained from the extra effort of grappling with the stiffer action. I had a feeling of impotence, as though I were a light bulb flickering from an uneven flow of current. Occasionally, I had to pick out, by ear, transitions from one section to another because of energy loss leading to memory lapses. This might have been avoided if my automatic controls had been more reliably imbedded and had taken over when other systems failed. But in the interim between the last recital and this one, I rather took the Chopin for granted, performing it for my own gratification, instead of practicing it slowly, daily.

In addition to all of this, I have to admit that I committed The Unpardonable: I forgot to remember to love the music.

* * *

It is always a difficult thing to know how to begin again after a recital. Here it is the Monday-morning-after, and I am sitting down to what amounts to doing my laundry. It is the image which comes from this laboriously slow and cleansing process; and if, indeed, there were a wash basin, I would probably see a ring around it from the soil created by too much performance and not enough practice. And what does this cleansing consist of? For example, in the Bach, at a very slow metronome setting, I am taking one movement at a time in sections, twice hands together, twice hands alone, then together again, etc., etc....purely technical without any emotional investment. Actually, it's a rather hypnotic process: with the old Seth Thomas metronome ticking monotonously back and forth, yet with a certain stolid support that is pacifying. The special value this rhythmic process has for a romantic piece like the Chopin, is that it irons out the creases of the old rubatos (by now, too licentious) and leaves it ready for fresh and discreet improvisation.

* * *

Today, on Beethoven's birthday, December 16th, I have a confession to make: my passion for him and his music is so unreasoned that I love people who love him even if I've never met them. When I read Donald Tovey's preface to the Urtext edition of the Sonatas, so full of tender reverence for the Master's every notation, I had an overwhelming desire to have known this man. I also wonder whether my closeness to Schumann is due, in part, to the fact (unknown to me until this evening) that we worship the same musical god. In Schumann's *On Music and Musicians,* there is a gorgeous expression of his feeling for Beethoven: "...this Beethoven in whom Nature simultaneously combined the gifts for which she usually requires a thousand vessels."

It is uncanny that the work which inspired these words of Schumann's was the Leonore Overture #3, the very same which moved me over a year ago to write a most passionate essay, into which I poured my last drop of love. While listening to this immortal overture today, it stuck me that the Florestan motif — a fragment of the beautiful aria he sings in the dungeon in the opera, *Fidelio,* is almost to the note, identical to the "Lebewohl" (Adieu) motif of "my" sonata, and is probably the reason I feel so drawn to it.

I think that there is an élite fraternity of those who know the truth: that Beethoven was the greatest genius who ever lived. The greatness of Schumann is magnified by his humble self-questioning: "Do you, too, dare to praise Beethoven?...to be so presumptuous?" But we allow ourselves the privilege because the self-indulgence of expression is so pleasurable.

* * *

This chapter will probably mark the all-time low-point of this Chronicle — at least I certainly hope that this is the worst. It is Wednesday, December 17th, I am faced with my heaviest schedule of teaching this afternoon; the house is way below my standards of orderliness, every corner seeming to cry out for attention; there is the laundry, dinner to prepare in advance before the lessons begin, Dennis' Music Department concert this evening. It is already 10 a.m. and I am nowhere near approaching the piano. So what am I doing about all of this? I am writing. I must sort myself out, because at this moment I simply do not feel equal to coping with the pressures upon me.

At rock bottom, I was only too willing to try anything that would get me out of the slump, in which I felt incapable of continuing this whole scene. My mother, an armchair nutritionist, diagnosed the situation as complete physical and nervous exhaustion. She returned within the hour and instead of chicken soup, she had "goodies," such as yeast, wheat germ, yogurt, Vitamin B complex, C's, etc., and whipped up a rather unpalatable concoction which, however, had me feeling revolutionally better in a very short time.

I have read, since, that violinist Yehudi Menuhin munches on similar fare backstage before concerts, from what he calls his "concert picnic-basket," and I can honestly state that rarely, since that low day when I changed my eating habits, did I suffer that feeling of physical or emotional impotence. We can obviously change our very outlook on life, dramatically, by keeping fit.

* * *

If there is anything which is as sensually satisfying to the touch as the keyboard these days, it is my dogs' heads. Probably the only interruption I do not resent and actually welcome, is a soft muzzle, and soulful eyes suddenly looking up at me from under the piano.

The flyers are here! They are surely the most fun fringe benefit of the whole deal. I have been allotted a juicy stack of 500 for myself, for private distribution; the remaining 2500 to be strategically deposited here and there for publicity, with a portion held back for use as programs at the concert. The immediate impulse is to give them out to friends, pupils, and relatives like hotcakes; but then it occurs to me that the stack will probably diminish in volume faster than I realize, and that these little throwaways might have to last a lifetime as the material evidence to myself that Carol Montparker, pianist, ever existed.

It was fun to choose the proof, the layout, the finish, the lettering, and quite amusing to juggle the words around to constitute a biography. "Amusing," because if I didn't let my sense of humor take over, it could have been destructive. The fact remains that my only "credentials" are that I can play. I have no memorable prizes or clippings to back me up or to create pre-impressions. For while others my age were flitting back and forth between Brussels, Warsaw, Moscow, Geneva, Paris, London, Toronto, to try and place in one of the coveted competitions, most of which are limited to younger people, I was raising babies.

It is, I think, an unfortunate situation that a late bloomer cannot find a single opportunity available when, if anything, the thirties represent a more fertile and ripe period for expression, and a better measure of the artist. The more youthful interpretations are ac-

CAROL MONT PARKER
PIANIST

CARNEGIE RECITAL HALL
MONDAY EVENING AT 8:00 ● FEBRUARY 9

CAROL MONT PARKER, pianist

CAROL MONT PARKER, New York-born pianist, majored in music at Queens College where she was the recipient of the Orchestral Society Award and featured soloist with the orchestra. She studied privately with the distinguished pedagogues and pianists Leopold Mittman and Josef Fidelman.

Ms. Parker has appeared in solo recital as well as in chamber ensembles throughout the New York area, and the southwest, and has been heard on radio programs of WNYC and WQXR. Among her engagements this season she is presenting a number of recitals at Hofstra University, Queens College and various other concert series in the Metropolitan area, all prior to her New York debut on February 9th at Carnegie Recital Hall.

PROGRAM

Partita I ....J. S. BACH
      Praeludium
      Allemande
      Courante
      Sarabande
      Menuet I - II - I
      Gigue

Sonata, Opus 81a, "Les Adieux" ....BEETHOVEN
      Adagio; Allegro (Les Adieux)
      Andante Espressivo (L'Absence)
      Vivacissimamente (Le Retour)

INTERMISSION

Etudes Symphoniques, Opus 13 ....SCHUMANN
      Theme et Variations

Ballade No. 4 in F minor, Opus 52 ....CHOPIN

STEINWAY PIANO

TICKETS: All seats $3.00. On sale at Carnegie Hall Box Office, 154 West 57th Street, New York, N.Y. 10019 two weeks in advance of concert. For mail orders, enclose a stamped, self-addressed envelope.

NEW YORK RECITAL ASSOCIATES
1776 Broadway at 57th Street • New York, N.Y. 10019

quired rather than experienced, and therefore more superficial. Very often the drive to gain fame as early as possible consumes itself. Instead of using a few years to increase repertoire, live life, love, reflect, the artist makes the rounds with whatever compositions are already under his fingers and uses them here and there until, before he knows it, he is stripped of material and may have to take a hiatus in his career to work. Sometimes the momentum can be lost and it becomes increasingly difficult to break in again. What I am trying to say is that people choose to live their lives in any of various patterns. The age limits to twenty-five are unrealistic and unfair, and I suspect they have discouraged and snuffed out many a talent, perhaps even some great talents, from ever entering the scene, a loss not only to the artist, but to the world.

* * *

My piano man, Wally Schreiber, is as much a doctor to me as any medical specialist could be. He is not only an expert technician with a super instinct about the guts of the instrument, but he has become a good friend, reliably and reassuringly there whenever the health of my piano needs his attention, (which is to say, my health, as well.) After a good strong cup of coffee, his only prerequisite, with a bit of nice, homey pianistic gossip thrown in, he settles down to a couple of hours of devoted fine tuning, including all sorts of bizarre and jarring soundings the purpose of which *I* can never understand.

Afterwards! There is a quiet spell of communication in which he is well aware of what the sound means to me, and I am once again enchanted by the refreshing joy of a perfectly tuned piano.

It is a joy which string players, for example, can never appreciate, being able to tune up each time they go to play, while a pianist must savor the diminishing moments as they last. Wally is the first man who could please even a fine string player's impeccable ear. It is when the piano is in complete accord with itself that the distinctive essence of the instrument is in full bloom to be appreciated, for the special ripeness and sensibility of its tone and timbre. And, needless to say, the quality of the performance is directly proportionate to the quality of the tool.

* * *

I am writing another letter to Artur Rubinstein this evening after his rare appearance on TV in a Chopin concerto as well as some solo pieces. He never ceases to amaze, inspire and fascinate me and I have long considered him as one of my great teachers. I want to again express gratitude and love, and to share with him the excitement of my upcoming New York recital. I think he will know me from my letter and the flyer which I will include. The reasons will be apparent after this story I have to tell.

Several years ago after an astoundingly beautiful Rubinstein recital in Huntington, New York, where we live, I wrote him my first letter, so carried away was I by the experience. I said *everything,* and it was truly a heart's flow which I hoped, yet doubted would reach him. Several months later at another one of his recitals, we were lucky enough to greet him backstage afterwards. I asked him whether he possibly had received a letter "from a lady named Carol Parker..." and he suddenly and eagerly quoted to me from my letter and said, "Are *you* Carol Parker? I loved and kept your letter! It struck a responsive chord inside me," whereupon he proceeded to start kissing me, first on one cheek then the other, and there ensued an animated conversation between my husband, Rubinstein, and myself. All the way home I plagued Guy with such questions as "How many times do you suppose he kissed me?"

Within the next few months the news was that Rubinstein was ill (with shingles). I sent off a letter and, under separate cover, two of my best watercolors as a get-well gift. Months went by, and then one day, out of the blue, I received a telegram: "Received your lovely letter belatedly. Please phone me tomorrow at the Chicago Sheraton Blackstone Hotel, (phone...) Affectionately, Artur Rubinstein." When I could stop shaking, a quick look at the date revealed that "tomorrow" meant today, so I dialed the number and my nervous tension was dispelled the moment the switchboard connected me to his room and I heard the throaty "Hello?"

I said "Hello, Mr. Rubinstein," and he said, "Is this Carol Parker?" He said he remembered quite well what I looked like from backstage, and we had what I could only describe as a lively, funny, beautiful half-hour of conversation as though we were old friends. We talked about the alliance between the arts, explaining why some people (myself included) often enjoy painting as well as playing. (He had not, at this point received the aquarelles; but after he did, I received a very gracious thank-you note). We talked about our respective spouses, his recent illness, his ideas about programming, and whether or not I had good seats for his next appearance at C.W. Post College. He asked me to phone him at the Drake Hotel in New York and he would put aside better tickets,...and then he said, "Now then, when am I going to kiss you again?" And the artist-clown dual personality continued joking until I was nearly limp with hysterics, extracting from me a promise that I meet him backstage, *beforehand*, at this forthcoming program, which I naturally did do! I feel privileged to have been granted a chance to know this venerable Artur Rubinstein.

I haven't written him since then, but with his phenomenal memory, even though he celebrates his eighty-ninth birthday in one month, perhaps he, too, will remember....

* * *

Human nature is so full of perversities. For four days I have been quaking with insecurity due to the lack of time and suitable atmosphere for practice with everyone home for the two weeks of Christmas vacation. The house has been abustle with phones ringing, friends visiting, and everybody off in different directions. The piano is right smack in the middle of the traffic pattern. Today I suddenly find myself with a spell of three hours of solitude, and I am not at all inclined to sit down and work. The head is fertile with notions to jot down, the stomach is hungry, and it's as though the piano is daring me not to come; it is so available that it has become almost unappealing. Obviously, I must avail myself of this precious time — the inspiration button must be pushed summoning up the necessary flow of juices, and so,...onward!

It is very easy to lose sight of the fact that I am giving these recitals because I want to and not because I have to. Whether it was a sub-conscious or conscious need or desire which precipitated the series of commitments, it was entirely my own doing. The malaise and work are self-imposed then, and although I would not use the word "suffering" simply because it has a maudlin sound, (even though it frequently amounts to that) I cannot even talk about this side of it or expect sympathy when it is obvious I asked for it.

So I have to focus again on the affirmative side of it. Indeed, I have to do this as a mental exercise, for whether it is a physical lack of energy or a low state of mind stemming from any number of other causes, my attitudes and confidence and then the playing suffer as a direct result. This much I know: that my physical and mental well-being are vital to the success of this entire venture.

An amazing, much-needed conversation just took place with a flutist friend who had a debut recital at Carnegie Recital Hall last season, and who recommended the agency that is managing my recital (N.Y. Recital Associates, run by the congenial and efficient Anne O'Donnell). The talk started with a cynical wisecrack from me referring to the nervous anticipation mounting up at this point, one month into the home stretch. With the cheeriest smile she said, "Carol, the whole thing is so much fun!" Then she reminded me of the fact that the entire hall will be filled to the brim with folks who are emitting nothing but positive rays of loving support — all my favorite people — the warmest of audiences. Furthermore, it's a lovely, hospitable, aesthetically pleasing room to play in.

One of the lovelier fringe benefits of this whole venture is that as a result of the wide distribution and mailing of the flyers to an endless list of places with which I'd virtually lost touch over the years, I am daily the happy recipient of notes of response and support, and greetings from past acquaintances many of whom are planning to attend on February 9th, which will make the event, among other things, a very happy reunion.

* * *

More than ever before in my life, I am experiencing the exhilaration that comes from utilizing one's entire potential. It is a great feeling. Along with this, there is an increasing certainty that my convictions were true: that one can have super-control over one's life, can increase its quality immeasurably, and should follow all impulses and carry them through because there is nothing that is totally impossible. I feel more in control (in all ways) than ever before.

Starting with the piano, obviously as a result of all the stepped-up and intense practice, I feel very much aware of the technical and artistic control, and I have brought myself up to new levels of pianism dormant these many years.

The chain of events involving the decision-making and the routine of preparation was full of steps: self-motivated, self-disciplined, self-perpetuating and promoting, etc. Basically, it is a three-part process — the urge, the discipline, the realization. The beautiful thing is that one step has directly led to another, and in the process I have been enjoying stimulating new acquaintances and enriched correspondence, and have branched out with new outlets. The writing is one good example of this, and the beginnings of an inkling, at this moment, that even others might find my scribblings of any interest, and that even this tangential manifestation of the entire experience may reap rewards, is a most happy notion. What's more, it feeds back into the playing.

* * *

There's a certain purely physical feeling of capability which comes into my hands sometimes and is very reassuring. It is a limber, facile, raring-to-go sensation which may express itself in restless flexing when away from the piano, or in dynamic, sparkling fingerwork when the keyboard is at hand. Other times, probably as a function of physical or mental fatigue, the impotence of the "flickering-light-bulb" syndrome sets in to haunt me. Or worse, I may wake up to find I have slept on my hand, and am plagued by a two-day sprain, or, once in a while an arthritic-type stiffness may threaten to hamper the dexterity.

All of these add up to just another in the long list of independent variables, upon which the success of the performance is based.

* * *

The most comforting thing I've read in the past few weeks is a quote of Casals: "The mere thought of a public performance is enough to give me a nightmare. I know of no other artist who is as tormented as I am with nerves." The knowledge that such as he have suffered too, and yet overcome and carry through on their high standards of quality, is just the reminder I need. I do not need to be told that nervous tension is "unnecessary," "unintelligent," "silly," "a function of lack of preparedness," "unprofessional," — any of that. I need the assurance that what I have come to accept as a fact-of-life about myself, is not necessarily destructive, nor uncommon, nor in any way related to quality.

* * *

Getting acquainted with the piano at Carnegie Recital Hall.

Carnegie Recital Hall must be one of the busiest spots in the city. One gets a sense of continuity from spending a couple of hours there. Placards get posted, placards get taken down, flyers get stuffed in the racks and are fingered and taken by browsers in the lobby; the room is booked solidly from morning till night with a stream of rehearsers and performers of all shapes, sizes and standards, climbing onto the stage, projecting their voices or their instruments to their own masses of fantasized or real audiences.

Today I quietly peeked in at a gifted young man forty minutes early for an important audition. At an appropriate break in his practicing, I told him that I had hoped to sneak in a try at the piano, and he suggested that even a three-minute stab at it would reveal a lot. So he generously relinquished a bit of his time to me and then we shared some impressions of the piano and the acoustics. (Subsequently, I was able to schedule two and a half hours for myself that afternoon.) Perhaps the one thing that is a purer joy than the actuality of a lovely hall like Carnegie Recital, filled with a breathing, expectant audience, a splendid nine-foot Steinway, spotlights, and a tingling feeling of sensitivity in the fingers, is...the empty hall, same piano, same good fingers, and the projected fantasy of the audience.

Today, with the unexpected pleasure of the two-plus hours alone in the hall, it was love at first sight between the piano and me, and I played until I ran out of steam. The resonance and tone were generally so lovely that I felt entirely comfortable and happy in front of the 300 velvety seats filled with my imaginary audience.

There is an amazing difference between the sound coming from a piano with that extra two feet in length, and other shorter instruments. We don't often get a chance to diddle around on one of these monsters and the omnipotent feeling is simply indescribable. It is that certain *quelque chose* which creates the great and memorable piano sounds we adore in concert, which linger in our ears and for which we strive at home, but can only come close to reproducing.

* * *

Sometimes after hearing a fine, sensitive performance or a brilliant one, by a pianist whose name I've never even heard of before, I realize how the world abounds in talent, and how expendable I am, . . . so why "bother"?

At other times, after hearing a particularly fine, sensitive or brilliant performance by myself (!), I realize how unique we each are, and how there is always a place for excellence and originality — which justify their own existence.

* * *

Curses! This routine of trying out one piano after another in the various recital places is wearing and frustrating. I have three dates within a week of each other, and am attempting to schedule practice sessions on the three instruments prior to the onslaught. Each, naturally, has its idiosyncracies, and remembering where and what they all are is tricky business. The Carnegie piano, I now know is lovely, and although it is not entirely without its little adjustments, I am really looking forward to it. Today's revelations, however, are very disheartening. Another thuddy, brittle sound, and a stiff new action. To consider this, in any way a rehearsal for the New York recital is insane. The piano is an entirely different species of beast from top to toe. It would not be far-fetched to liken the difference between the two actions to the depth of nap on fabrics; one could compare it to letting one's fingers sink into the deep pile of a rich velvet, and then gliding along on a shiny satin surface.

One time at Josef's, bemoaning the fact that I failed to bring out an inner voice in the profound opening of the Beethoven, I was quick to blame it on the easier action of his old Mason and Hamlin. Almost angrily, he said, "It doesn't matter *any* instrument, the same thumb is going to play it!"

The redeeming side of the situation, (the inspiration derived from an unique new instrument with its own distinctiveness) is completely missing in my next (third) recital piano. The piano should meet the artist half-way — the sound should step out to be shaped by the pianist, and not have to be drawn out as it will be in this case. Another annoyance is that what the performer hears up on the stage in this hall, is not at all the same as what reaches the audience. They hear a much fuller sound, and the inclination is to force for a bigger tone when it isn't even necessary.

* * *

What is the magic of the *N.Y. Times* that the appearance of one's name in BLOCK LETTERS in an ad that one pays for oneself, can, nevertheless, be so exciting? That concert page, like a counterpane of assorted sized boxes filled with some of the most illustrious names, shoulder to shoulder with the "unknowns," is like a joyous tintinnabulation of all the various concerts being played at once — proclaiming themselves and clamoring to be heard.

* * *

I arrived this evening with just enough time to warm up a bit on the piano before the audience began to file into this lovely community recital hall. But instead, I found the tuner frantically racing against time to meet the deadline, with a reassuring aside to me: "I hate these high pressure jobs, and will no way be able to do a de-

cent tuning on this piano tonight, lady, no matter how hard I try." Comforting. There must be an element of humor in there somewhere.

So here I am again sitting in a lounge where they put me to await recital time, and I feel somewhat as though I am about to be wheeled in to surgery. I am running through my repertoire of calming tricks, the writing, the crosswords, etc., yet the hands will not stop shaking.

What I am about to describe is, to me, a beautiful success story: I decided to take the bull by the horns and give the meditation another go-round. By consciously relaxing my body from the toes up to the head, breathing deeply, and saying a mantra to myself on each exhalation, I achieved a remarkable repose within about three minutes. After another few minutes, I imposed the images of Bernstein and Rubinstein in their joyful music-making into my mind, and the notion of "Certainly, this is what it's all about" took over. I walked out onto the stage with a genuinely warm and happy smile, and without shaking at all, for the first time, I was in complete control from the very outset when I started to play. What's more, the playing was more relaxed and better than ever. I didn't even suffer with the abominable sniffing. It was a definite turning point for me, as I had begun to think of myself as a hopelessly habitual victim of nerves with no way out.

The finest accolade of the evening came from my son Dennis. In the car on the way home from this pre-recital, I apologized to the three sensitive musicians (who happened to comprise my family) — that they have had to attend and abide the same program not only in the several concerts, but at home, and yet have only offered valid and constructive advice as well as loving support. Dennis said, "Don't apologize, Mom. When you play like you did tonight, it's as though I am hearing the music for the first time."

* * *

Probably it is the child in me which makes me take the day after a recital completely off, and reward myself by buying something frivolous and pretty, which I don't need at all. But afterwards, there is always, again, the difficulty of forcing myself back to the discipline to reset the gears of practice into motion. Just as a garment will have creases after being worn, a program, too, after performance, inevitably shows signs of wear.

* * *

Almost daily, someone is likely to allude to the fact that I am wearing several hats and ask me, in complete stupefaction, how in the world I am managing to pull off the preparation for this mammoth show and continuing to function as the maid, the chauffeur, the teacher, the cook, the wife and mother. I would most happily accept any compliment thrown my way regarding how super-efficient, wondrously competent and remarkable I might be, but the truth is, that I, myself, do not now consider it such a coup; (or perhaps I had better reserve commentary until after February 9th).

I think we are all guilty of wanton time-wasting if not life-wasting. I do not include relaxing in this category, but there are innumerable things that I was doing prior to my decision, which were extraneous, meaningless, mere functions of habit, and voracious consumers of my time and energies. It doesn't matter what these things were. But I have gathered together the unruly wisps of time and compiled them into an embarrassingly large parcel — and now the difference is, that my day is an austere, carefully budgeted one; but when the evening comes, I have a generally good feeling that I have accomplished something which is important to me, without sacrificing. If I had to forego or neglect my other responsibilities, I am sure I would suffer guilt and severe inner conflict which would take the edge off the pleasures of self-fulfillment.

As I implied before, I don't mind a pat on the back if I am managing the domestic side of my life without too many snags these days. However, the last thing I want to have happen, is to have my playing judged by any standard or extra consideration other than those pertaining directly to the pianism. Years ago, we heard an excellent recital presented by a business friend who was a fine pianist. The caption over the *N. Y. Times* review was not only unfair but unfunny. It read, "Ad-man Gives Recital." My goal is certainly not to be praised for a fine job I might do considering I am a full-time homemaker, etc. as well.

* * *

It is one week before C-Day and Josef wanted me to come over and run through the program for him. All my instincts bristled against the idea at this point, no matter how reassuring, loving, and musically valuable his influence has always been. Instead I visited with him and had a few hours of delightful conversation without one note being struck. I was carried off to the Berlin of the 1920s where one single town square had windows opening out onto it out of which poured the pianistic efforts of Claudio Arrau, Vladimir Horowitz, Josef Fidelman, and Leopold Mittman — all at once! On and on went the tales from the Hochschüle with names like Kreutzer, Lili Kraus, Gieseking, Steinberg, Szell and Serkin, and accounts of the concert tours and competitions such as the most highly coveted Blüthner Prize won by both Fidelman and Mittman in their turn, the prize consisting of a beautiful Blüthner piano. Both gentlemen were able to ship their beloved instruments to America in spite of their hardships of resettlement. The complete immersion of the conservatory life in Europe with its artistic ferment, intensive study and élite society, has nothing to equal it anymore, anywhere. We have to be content to enjoy, vicariously, the second-hand strands which are passed down to us, and I am insatiably greedy to absorb as much of that scene as I can.

* * *

Having been somewhat cloistered all winter in a somewhat hibernative state with my piano I have been virtually oblivious to external effects such as the news of the world and weather changes. However, even the thick physical and intellectual walls were not impervious to today's store of natural phenomena: another in a series of severe winter zero-degree snowstorms. Only this time, we have an electrical power failure and are without heat or hot water. The schools are closed, the kids are trying to keep warm, and I have been trying to practice wearing three sweaters which render my arms into overstuffed sausages but do nothing at all for the icicles which were my fingers.

* * *

At the college where my last pre-recital is scheduled (this week), there is a most unaccommodating chap who finds himself with awesome power as Custodian of the Key to the Piano. After giving me a song and dance about security precautions, he had to be practically kowtowed to before he relinquished said key, (despite instructions from the Music Department), thus reducing my scant one-and-a-half hours of necessary orientation, by half.

Someday I am going to write a book called "Pianos I've Known," and today's specimen will go down as the Dead Middle. The last two pianos were "Avis' " (in other words, not Steinway's). But this nine-footer, a Steinway belonging to the college, is an oldie that has been through the wars. The panel behind the keyboard is literally gouged to bits by the passionate fingernails of hundreds of pianists, and the instrument has undergone major surgery on its innards. In spite of its rich, full bass, and bell-like upper treble, one must squeeze to get any juice out of the middle registers. The interesting development to me, though, is that I am now so much more secure, technically, that the instruments no longer seem like bucking broncos to be broken or conquered, and I can stay with it and make music with whatever is in there.

* * *

At this, final pre-recital, I graduated from mere performing artist to Chief Stagehand.

When I arrived at the college's recital hall one hour early for a warm-up, there was a lecture in progress in the room, but no one else in sight. (I did not warm up, but am now an expert on the differences between "seraphim and cherubim.") A half-hour before the scheduled recital, there was still no one around, so I had to push the nine-foot baby across the stage myself and try to locate, through trial and error, the button to lower the curtain behind the piano so that the backdrop would not be the vast arena of stage with its ladders, cables, and theatrical paraphernalia. What's more, the building was entirely unheated. The professor had been lecturing with his coat on to a class of students with their coats on. My audience kept bundled while I, wearing a thin dress, (having found the stage lights devastatingly hot during my last recital), played with an arctic draught blowing on my back. The rest rooms were locked (!), and the lighting was entirely inadequate. I was unable to figure out the complex panel of switches, so I carried on in semi-dusk, with weird patterns of interlacing shadows competing for my attention across the keyboard. Now, I can play in darkness at home, relaxed, but under pressure, it is quite a different story. When I finally decided I had better begin, the people never stopped pouring in, with the rear door slamming open and shut through the entire Bach Partita in the most anarchic, distracting recital set-up imaginable.

I kept trying to focus in on the humor, but truthfully it eluded me this time. It was an utterly inhospitable way in which to welcome an artist to a recital place — unacceptable even to me, who could never be classified as a prima donna type. This series of atrocities seemed to me almost a conspiracy. My mind was plagued throughout the program by obsessive, recurrent thoughts that I would have to stop, or that I would develop pneumonia before Monday evening arrived (Carnegie), and that I certainly would never make it to the end, and yet, somehow, I did.

Practicing on stage in empty Carnegie Recital Hall.

There are two faint flickers of value from yesterday's fiasco: the first is the pleasure of knowing I did it in spite of everything; the second, in the form of a little old lady who approached me hesitatingly for an autograph with the excuse, "You never know...you may even be famous one day."

*　*　*

It is as though I can see the grains of sand relentlessly dropping through the hourglass three days before Carnegie, and thoughts of how the time would be best spent, and am I truly well-enough prepared, are constantly with me.

*　*　*

Two days to zero-hour. We went in today to Carnegie Recital Hall for my scheduled practice sessions, and my first impressions were, happily, reconfirmed: the piano is lovely and completely well-suited to me. The acoustics are as fine as any hall I've ever been in and the room has an old-world elegance about it — the velvety draperies and seats, the curved moldings with floral motifs, all sadly lacking in the newer sterile halls. The best thing about the day was that everything played by itself, and the family, whose taste, honesty and musical instincts I truly respect, kept coming across with the most positive, fervent assurances that the whole thing sounded "wonderful," and that I had "nothing to worry about." At this moment, I am tremendously excited by the prospect ahead.

* * *

The day before. Telephone calls are coming in all day long from well-wishers, some from across the country, and one from Haiti; telegrams, including a cable from Sweden; flowers in advance; I feel so expectant, it's almost as though I were about to have a baby! (As long as I don't lay an egg.)

* * *

Today. February 9th. I don't know how to discuss brain waves or brain activity in intelligent, scientific terms, but if they have a gauge to measure it, mine would certainly register over the deep end. I feel supercharged electronically. My stream-of-consciousness is dragging me through every human mood from the most fearsome insecurity to the most cocky sureness, and back down again. The roller coaster ride is no fun at all.

* * *

The perspective I have today, February 10th, is obviously quite different from that which I shall have, say, in a month or a year from now. My thoughts are barely coherent and certainly not cohesive. The main thing is, I have a happy feeling of fulfillment inside of me, entirely independent of others' responses, with only a curiosity about the review. It is how I would have hoped to feel.

* * *

My first glimpse of Carnegie last evening after the long and tense drive was almost surrealistic. The marquee of the Great Carnegie and the elegant, canopied entrance to the Recital Hall seemed more brilliantly illuminated and grander than ever. I dashed across 57th Street in my blue jeans and pea-jacket, with my black velvet formal ensemble and white silk blouse flapping wildly on the hanger, and stopped short on the way in to grin secretly at my poster in the showcase at the entrance, under the sign which read "TONIGHT."

My one thought was to get to the piano, the only balm for my tormented nervous system. The magical transformation from hippie to refined-lady-concert-pianist having been accomplished with 3/4 of an hour to spare, I flew to the stage, and as I knew it would, the tension was dispelled with the first few tones from that beautiful piano, my friend. Not long afterwards, Josef's reassuring face appeared, and his enthusiasm for how it was sounding topped off the thrilling sensation of potential that was within me — as long as I was seated there. But then came his admonitions that I must not tire myself, and I had to relinquish my security and begin the lonely backstage vigil for the half-hour remaining. In spite of everyone's touchingly frantic and unsubtle efforts to cheer and distract me, and in spite of

The placard at the entrance of Carnegie Recital Hall
on night of performance.

telegrams and bouquets arriving and all manner of behind-the-scenes activity of stagehands, manager, etc., on came the inevitable rush of symptoms. The atmosphere this time was not at all conducive to meditation. I tried.

By now, I have described the array of nervous disorders which plague me before recitals. I will not give a blow-by-blow account this time except to say that "they" were all present with bells on, and then some. And when, finally, the stagehand said, "Any time you are ready, I will dim the lights," robot-like I answered, "Now."

Remarkable — how we manage to project confidence, enjoyment, ease, delight, and polish, when, in fact, it was only by the most gargantuan efforts that the nerves were overcome, as I felt myself the focal point of every ear, eye, and antenna in the room. The toll I feel most dramatically today, even as I am writing. I want very much to have the immediacy of my responses in this Chronicle, and yet I am almost too enervated to record them.

So! I somehow played even better than I'd hoped. Josef says, "There is no limit to 'better.' Say 'thank you' for what was." In this case there was plenty to be thankful for.

The Concert, February 9, 1976.

Although I had to begin the Bach with a strange, new neuritis-like pins-and-needles sensation which decided to develop in my right hand five minutes before I came out on stage, by some miracle the Partita flowed right along and I was able to savor and enjoy the distinctive differences between each dance movement which makes this composition such a delectable salad for the first course of a program.

I would never have the audacity to rate my Beethoven in terms of how it communicated itself to others. I can only say I was deeply involved, I felt I successfully expressed my own feelings about it, and I was grateful that the technical problems never imposed themselves between me and the music. I will venture to say that I think the joyousness of Le Retour, the last movement, was infectiously transmitted to the audience, borne out by their most enthusiastic response at the conclusion.

I have described how I feel about the Schumann in previous pages. It did not let me down. It is universally appealing, I love it, probably I conveyed this love.

The Chopin, I felt more personally than ever in this performance. I wasn't even tired, somehow, by the demanding last pages, so I was able to squeeze the last drop out in a momentum which seemed to have carried me along from the first note of the recital.

I was aware of the electricity in the air between my audience (a full house!) and me throughout the evening. During the recital portion, very little impressed itself upon me (a face here, a rustling there), except for my involvement with the music and the joyousness of performing it. The duration of the program seemed, towards the end, to be bitterly short, although as programs go this one might be considered on the long side.

The wisps of images following the playing amount to a sort of tissue collage. There were the usual pleasures such as the flowers (tons of them!), "Bravas," encores, a beautiful reception at the Recital Hall during which I was buoyed up and whirled through a triumphant eddy of greetings and congratulations, beautiful family, beautiful friends, beautiful Russian Tea Room, beautiful, intimate ride home with the family ... a beautiful evening, of course.

As Dennis reminded me in the car on the way to the Hall, "As of tomorrow morning, Mom, you're an ordinary citizen just like the rest of us ... no special treatment ..." I am more than happy and relieved to accept my new status and go merrily about the business of decompressing.

I am aware of major transformations within me as a result of the life style I imposed upon myself. Supreme among these is that I was forced upon myself and grew to enjoy my own company a lot more. I have developed a deep sense of contentment, but have a much lower tolerance level for life-wasting. These austere months of preparation have given me a keen appreciation and respect for the precious commodity: time, and a need, (which is almost greed), to expend mine as economically as possible. Perhaps I have grown up a little.

With all the positive, relieved, happy feelings, there is also, naturally, a sense of loss, similar to the feeling I get when I have read the last paragraph of a great novel which has engrossed me over a period of time. My innermost thoughts, however, which I will not ponder more deeply, nor tune into finer focus in these pages, concern the joys and achievements and their relative position and balance in the hierarchy of priorities in my life as a whole. As far as this Chronicle concerns itself, the curtain is down.

* * *

Each morning since Tuesday, we have made the increasingly anticlimactic pilgrimage down the driveway to The Puddle into which our *New York Times* is delivered daily. The following review is reprinted from the Sunday paper for whatever it may or may not be worth.

Music in Review

Piano Skill Shown By Carol Parker

Too many young musicians make debuts while their training is still underdone, but there was nothing half-baked about the recital of Carol Mont Parker at Carnegie Recital Hall on Monday night. Miss Parker, a graduate of Queens College who has studied with Leopold Mittman and Josef Fidelman, put on an engrossing demonstration, particularly in Schumann's knuckle-cracking "Symphonic Etudes" and only a little less impressively in Bach's Partita No. 1 in B-flat Beethoven's "Les Adieux" Sonata and Chopin's Ballade No. 4 in F minor.

Miss Parker's technical polish stood her in good stead in the Schumann with its clotted chords and exhausting runs, and she went somewhat beyond pure duty by inserting two of the five posthumous études just before the formidable finale. She hit the mark best in bravura pages, with forceful, clean playing, and left most to be desired when blitheness might have been appropriate or, as in the Beethoven slow movement, a mood of tender sentiment.

Interpretatively, that is, Miss Parker's performances were sometimes a bit overly aggressive and splashy, as debut performances tend to be. But there was rarely a feeling of rote playing: the music moved in pliant expressive phrases, and breathed naturally. There was good independence of hands in the Bach Partita, as well as a strong pulse, rhythmic bounce and, occasionally, Gouldish tempos that the pianist handled without strain. Subtlety and variety of touch also marked Miss Parker's Bach, though she managed to sustain the suggestion of harpsichord style and sonority throughout.

All in all, a splendid debut by a pianist who needs only to let warmth and individuality shine through more clearly in her playing. As it is, Miss Parker starts where many young pianists leave off.

DONAL HENAHAN

POSTSCRIPT

Looking retrospectively over the eight years elapsed since the debut recital, the ways in which that whole episode has changed my life are clear to see. I have managed, for the most part, to sustain the precious established patterns of morning work hours, so there will be no going to seed; in fact Time has been kept rather scrupulously under control. There are solo and chamber recitals whenever the spirit moves me, and the joyful side of the playing has finally triumphed over the disagreeable elements which, though ever-present, are now easily dominated. It is probable that there will be more New York recitals.

The most startling awareness of change and time comes from re-reading one's own definitive statements such as "There is an elite fraternity who *know* Beethoven to be the greatest," which smack of the harmless arrogance borne of youthful ardor; perhaps it is possible to return, eventually, full-circle to this view. At the moment, however, having been a closet-Schubert pianist for years, I am venturing forth with caution and great reverence for his music — at the same time giving full rein to my lifelong passion for Brahms solo and chamber music.

With an ironic twist, the Chronicle has led, tangentially, into a preoccupation which has become an end in itself, sapping energy and time from the piano: writing. On the other hand, because of the writing — on mostly musical subjects — meetings and conversations with fascinating artists have in turn nourished the playing.

A major change in my personal life has made me keenly aware of the close relationship between one's inner harmony and peace and the ability to work well. Indeed, now happier than ever before, I wonder whether I would have needed to write a Chronicle had the recital taken place this year.

Finally, I am truly convinced it is possible, by living creatively, to arrange a composite of one's highest priorities and goals and to realize every one of them.

*   *   *   *   *   *